Julie,   1 Jun 2001

You told me you've been reading "classic" literature A-Z. I know you got as far as "C" with Cervantes. Here's an author from "D" for you to enjoy.

Jana Bryant

A Murmur in the Trees

Also available:

Odes to Common Things
   by Pablo Neruda

Odes to Opposites
   by Pablo Neruda

The Rose Window and Other Verse from New Poems
   by Rainer Maria Rilke

A Murmur in the Trees

Emily Dickinson

Selected and Illustrated by Ferris Cook

A Bulfinch Press Book

Little, Brown and Company

Boston · New York · Toronto · London

First Edition

LIBRARY OF CONGRESS CATALOGING-IN-PUBLICATION DATA

Dickinson, Emily, 1830–1886
     A murmur in the trees / Emily Dickinson : selected and illustrated
by Ferris Cook. — 1st ed.
       p.   cm.
     "A Bulfinch Press book."
     ISBN 0–8212–2500–6
     I. Cook, Ferris.   II. Title
PS1541.A6   1998
811'.4–dc21   97–40413

Bulfinch Press is an imprint and trademark of
Little, Brown and Company (Inc.)
Published simultaneously in Canada by
Little, Brown & Company (Canada) Limited

PRINTED IN THE UNITED STATES OF AMERICA

For my first friends:
Janet Smayda, Cathy Shallenberger,
Emily Whiting, Kathleen Bennett,
and Barbara Morrison

Contents

She slept beneath a tree— 15

Summer for thee, grant I may be 16

Nobody knows this little Rose— 17

Like her the Saints retire, 18

Papa above! 19

Some Rainbow—coming from the Fair! 20

So from the mould 21

New feet within my garden go— 22

A science—so the Savants say, 23

Will there really be a "Morning"? 24

Artists wrestled here! 25

Pigmy seraphs—gone astray— 26

An altered look about the hills— 27

For every Bird a Nest— 28

Except to Heaven, she is nought. 29

A feather from the Whippoorwill 30

Tho' my destiny be Fustian— 31

A *Wounded* Deer—leaps highest— 32

A fuzzy fellow, without feet, 33

I'm the little "Heart's Ease"! 34

An awful Tempest mashed the air— 35

With thee, in the Desert— 36

Did the Harebell loose her girdle 37

Over the fence— 38

I'm Nobody! Who are you? 39

While Asters— 40

I know a place where Summer strives 41

It will be Summer—eventually. 42

Through the Dark Sod—as Education— 43

A Murmur in the Trees—to note—   44
Good Morning—Midnight—   45
The Moon is distant from the Sea—   46
'Tis customary as we part   47
God made a little Gentian—   48
Civilization—spurns—the Leopard!   49
Within my Garden, rides a Bird   50
She sights a Bird—she chuckles—   51
To hear an Oriole sing   52
The Black Berry—wears a Thorn in his side—   53
She hideth Her the last—   54
A Dying Tiger—moaned for Drink—   55
Of Brussels—it was not—   56
The Spider holds a Silver Ball   57
You'll know Her—by Her Foot—   58
She dwelleth in the Ground—   59
I could bring You Jewels—had I a mind to   60
The Judge is like the Owl—   61
No Bobolink—reverse His Singing   62
The Robin is the One   63
Nature and God—I neither knew   64
Split the Lark—and you'll find the Music—   65
Because the Bee may blameless hum   66
As the Starved Maelstrom laps the Navies   67
Ribbons of the Year—   68
Drab Habitation of Whom?   69
Absent Place—an April Day—   70
A narrow Fellow in the Grass   71
The Leaves like Women interchange   72
I was a Phoebe—nothing more—   73
His Bill an Auger is   74
Bee! I'm expecting you!   75
Her little Parasol to lift   76
What Twigs We held by—   77

Like Men and Women Shadows walk   78
These are the Nights that Beetles love   79
A Spider sewed at Night   80
Alone and in a Circumstance   81
A prompt—executive Bird is the Jay—   82
A little Dog that wags his tail   83
A Sparrow took a Slice of Twig   84
The Clover's simple Fame   85
The Butterfly's Assumption Gown   86
I worked for chaff and earning Wheat   87
The Spider as an Artist   88
'Twas later when the summer went   89
The Way to know the Bobolink   90
The Mushroom is the Elf of Plants—   91
Pink—small—and punctual—   92
A Bee his burnished Carriage   93
A Rat surrendered here   94
A single Clover Plank   95
The Rat is the concisest Tenant.   96
The long sigh of the Frog   97
Lay this Laurel on the One   98
After all Birds have been investigated and laid aside—   99
The fairest Home I ever knew   100
The Gentian has a parched Corolla—   101
A Dew sufficed itself—   102
How soft a Caterpillar steps—   103
A Route of Evanescence   104
Before you thought of Spring   105
One of the ones that Midas touched   106
A winged spark doth soar about—   107
The Robin is a Gabriel   108
It came his turn to beg—   109
Its little Ether Hood   110
An Antiquated Tree   111

The Dandelion's pallid tube   112
His oriental heresies   113
Follow wise Orion   114
Come show thy Durham Breast   115
No Brigadier throughout the Year   116
Forever honored be the Tree   117
The Bat is dun, with wrinkled Wings–   118
The farthest Thunder that I heard   119
The Bobolink is gone–   120
Apparently with no surprise   121
The Pedigree of Honey   122
The Jay his Castanet has struck   123
A Cap of Lead across the sky   124
Sweet is the swamp with its secrets,   125
To make a prairie it takes a clover and one bee,   126

EMILY DICKINSON (1830–1886) was born in Amherst, Massachusetts, and is considered to be one of the greatest poets of American literature. The daughter of a prominent lawyer, she spent most of her life in her birthplace, gradually withdrawing from local activities, and spending her later years as a virtual recluse in her father's house. She composed over seventeen hundred unique lyrics dealing with religion, love, nature, death, and immortality, only seven of which were published during her lifetime. Her verse, noted for its aphoristic style, its wit, its delicate metrical variation, and its bold and startling imagery, has had great influence on twentieth-century poetry.

The Poems

25

She slept beneath a tree—
Remembered but by me.
I touched her Cradle mute—
She recognized the foot—
Put on her carmine suit
        And see!

31

Summer for thee, grant I may be
When Summer days are flown!
Thy music still, when Whippoorwill
And Oriole—are done!

For thee to bloom, I'll skip the tomb
And row my blossoms o'er!
Pray gather me—
        Anemone—
Thy flower—forevermore!

35

Nobody knows this little Rose—
It might a pilgrim be
Did I not take it from the ways
And lift it up to thee.
Only a Bee will miss it—
Only a Butterfly,
Hastening from far journey—
On its breast to lie—
Only a Bird will wonder—
Only a Breeze will sigh—
Ah Little Rose—how easy
For such as thee to die!

Like her the Saints retire,
In their Chapeaux of fire,
Martial as she!

Like her the Evenings steal
Purple and Cochineal
After the Day!

"Departed"—both—they say!
i.e. gathered away,
Not found,

Argues the Aster still—
Reasons the Daffodil
Profound!

61

Papa above!
Regard a Mouse
O'erpowered by the Cat!
Reserve within thy kingdom
A "Mansion" for the Rat!

Snug in seraphic Cupboards
To nibble all the day,
While unsuspecting Cycles
Wheel solemnly away!

Some Rainbow—coming from the Fair!
Some Vision of the World Cashmere—
I confidently see!
Or else a Peacock's purple Train
Feather by feather—on the plain
Fritters itself away!

The dreamy Butterflies bestir!
Lethargic pools resume the whir
Of last year's sundered tune!
From some old Fortress on the sun
Baronial Bees—march—one by one—
In murmuring platoon!

The Robins stand as thick today
As flakes of snow stood yesterday—
On fence—and Roof—and Twig!
The Orchis binds her feather on
For her old lover—Don the Sun!
Revisiting the Bog!

Without Commander! Countless! Still!
The Regiments of Wood and Hill
In bright detachment stand!
Behold! Whose Multitudes are these?
The children of whose turbaned seas—
Or what Circassian Land?

So from the mould
Scarlet and Gold
Many a Bulb will rise−
Hidden away, cunningly,
From sagacious eyes.

So from Cocoon
Many a Worm
Leap so Highland gay,
Peasants like me,
Peasants like Thee
Gaze perplexedly!

99

New feet within my garden go—
New fingers stir the sod—
A Troubadour upon the Elm
Betrays the solitude.

New children play upon the green—
New Weary sleep below—
And still the pensive Spring returns—
And still the punctual snow!

A science—so the Savants say,
"Comparative Anatomy"—
By which a single bone—
Is made a secret to unfold
Of some rare tenant of the mold,
Else perished in the stone—

So to the eye prospective led,
This meekest flower of the mead
Upon a winter's day,
Stands representative in gold
Of Rose and Lily, manifold,
And countless Butterfly!

Will there really be a "Morning"?
Is there such a thing as "Day"?
Could I see it from the mountains
If I were as tall as they?

Has it feet like Water lilies?
Has it feathers like a Bird?
Is it brought from famous countries
Of which I have never heard?

Oh some Scholar! Oh some Sailor!
Oh some Wise Man from the skies!
Please to tell a little Pilgrim
Where the place called "Morning" lies!

Artists wrestled here!
Lo, a tint Cashmere!
Lo, a Rose!
Student of the Year!
For the easel here
Say Repose!

Pigmy seraphs—gone astray—
Velvet people from Vevay—
Belles from some lost summer day—
Bees exclusive Coterie—

Paris could not lay the fold
Belted down with Emerald—
Venice could not show a cheek
Of a tint so lustrous meek—
Never such an Ambuscade
As of briar and leaf displayed
For my little damask maid—

I had rather wear her grace
Than an Earl's distinguished face—
I had rather dwell like her
Than be "Duke of Exeter"—
Royalty enough for me
To subdue the Bumblebee.

An altered look about the hills—
A Tyrian light the village fills—
A wider sunrise in the morn—
A deeper twilight on the lawn—
A print of a vermillion foot—
A purple finger on the slope—
A flippant fly upon the pane—
A spider at his trade again—
An added strut in Chanticleer—
A flower expected everywhere—
An axe shrill singing in the woods—
Fern odors on untravelled roads—
All this and more I cannot tell—
A furtive look you know as well—
And Nicodemus' Mystery
Receives its annual reply!

For every Bird a Nest—
Wherefore in timid quest
Some little Wren goes seeking round—

Wherefore when boughs are free—
Households in every tree—
Pilgrim be found?

Perhaps a home too high—
Ah Aristocracy!
The little Wren desires—

Perhaps of twig so fine—
Of twine e'en superfine,
Her pride aspires—

The Lark is not ashamed
To build upon the ground
Her modest house—

Yet who of all the throng
Dancing around the sun
Does so rejoice?

Except to Heaven, she is nought.
Except for Angels—lone.
Except to some wide-wandering Bee
A flower superfluous blown.

Except for winds—provincial.
Except by Butterflies
Unnoticed as a single dew
That on the Acre lies.

The smallest Housewife in the grass,
Yet take her from the Lawn
And somebody has lost the face
That made Existence—Home!

A feather from the Whippoorwill
That everlasting—sings!
Whose galleries—are Sunrise—
Whose Opera—the Springs—
Whose Emerald Nest the Ages spin
Of mellow—murmuring thread—
Whose Beryl Egg, what Schoolboys hunt
In "Recess"—Overhead!

163

Tho' my destiny be Fustian—
Hers be damask fine—
Tho' she wear a silver apron—
I, a less divine—

Still, my little Gypsy being
I would far prefer,
Still, my little sunburnt bosom
To her Rosier,

For, when Frosts, their punctual fingers
On her forehead lay,
You and I, and Dr. Holland,
Bloom Eternally!

Roses of a steadfast summer
In a steadfast land,
Where no Autumn lifts her pencil—
And no Reapers stand!

A *Wounded* Deer—leaps highest—
I've heard the Hunter tell—
'Tis but the Ecstasy of *death*—
And then the Brake is still!

The *Smitten* Rock that gushes!
The *trampled* Steel that springs!
A Cheek is always redder
Just where the Hectic stings!

Mirth is the Mail of Anguish—
In which it Cautious Arm,
Lest anybody spy the blood
And "you're hurt" exclaim!

173

A fuzzy fellow, without feet,
Yet doth exceeding run!
Of velvet, is his Countenance,
And his Complexion, dun!

Sometime, he dwelleth in the grass!
Sometime, upon a bough,
From which he doth descend in plush
Upon the Passer-by!

All this in summer.
But when winds alarm the Forest Folk,
He taketh *Damask* Residence—
And struts in sewing silk!

Then, finer than a Lady,
Emerges in the spring!
A Feather on each shoulder!
You'd scarce recognize him!

By Men, yclept Caterpillar!
By me! But who am I,
To tell the pretty secret
Of the Butterfly!

I'm the little "Heart's Ease"!
I don't care for pouting skies!
If the Butterfly delay
Can I, therefore, stay away?

If the Coward Bumble Bee
In his chimney corner stay,
I, must resoluter be!
Who'll apologize for me?

Dear, Old fashioned, little flower!
Eden is old fashioned, too!
Birds are antiquated fellows!
Heaven does not change her blue.
Nor will I, the little Heart's Ease—
Ever be induced to do!

An awful Tempest mashed the air—
The clouds were gaunt, and few—
A Black—as of a Spectre's Cloak
Hid Heaven and Earth from view.

The creatures chuckled on the Roofs—
And whistled in the air—
And shook their fists—
And gnashed their teeth—
And swung their frenzied hair.

The morning lit—the Birds arose—
The Monster's faded eyes
Turned slowly to his native coast—
And peace—was Paradise!

209

With thee, in the Desert—
With thee in the thirst—
With thee in the Tamarind wood—
Leopard breathes—at last!

213

Did the Harebell loose her girdle
To the lover Bee
Would the Bee the Harebell *hallow*
Much as formerly?

Did the "Paradise"−persuaded−
Yield her moat of pearl−
Would the Eden *be* an Eden,
Or the Earl−an *Earl?*

Over the fence—
Strawberries—grow—
Over the fence—
I could climb—if I tried, I know—
Berries are nice!

But—if I stained my Apron—
God would certainly scold!
Oh, dear,—I guess if He were a Boy—
He'd—climb—if He could!

288

I'm Nobody! Who are you?
Are you—Nobody—Too?
Then there's a pair of us?
Don't tell! they'd advertise—you know!

How dreary—to be—Somebody!
How public—like a Frog—
To tell one's name—the livelong June—
To an admiring Bog!

While Asters—
On the Hill—
Their Everlasting fashions—set—
And Covenant Gentians—Frill!

337

I know a place where Summer strives
With such a practised Frost—
She—each year—leads her Daisies back—
Recording briefly—"Lost"—

But when the South Wind stirs the Pools
And struggles in the lanes—
Her Heart misgives Her, for Her Vow—
And she pours soft Refrains

Into the lap of Adamant—
And spices—and the Dew—
That stiffens quietly to Quartz—
Upon her Amber Shoe—

It will be Summer—eventually.
Ladies—with parasols—
Sauntering Gentlemen—with Canes—
And little Girls—with Dolls—

Will tint the pallid landscape—
As 'twere a bright Bouquet—
Tho' drifted deep, in Parian—
The Village lies—today—

The Lilacs—bending many a year—
Will sway with purple load—
The Bees—will not despise the tune—
Their Forefathers—have hummed—

The Wild Rose—redden in the Bog—
The Aster—on the Hill
Her everlasting fashion—set—
And Covenant Gentians—frill—

Till Summer folds her miracle—
As Women—do—their Gown—
Or Priests—adjust the Symbols—
When Sacrament—is done—

Through the Dark Sod—as Education—
The Lily passes sure—
Feels her white foot—no trepidation—
Her faith—no fear—

Afterward—in the Meadow—
Swinging her Beryl Bell—
The Mold-life—all forgotten—now—
In Ecstasy—and Dell—

416

A Murmur in the Trees—to note—
Not loud enough—for Wind—
A Star—not far enough to seek—
Nor near enough—to find—

A long—long Yellow—on the Lawn—
A Hubbub—as of feet—
Not audible—as Ours—to Us—
But dapperer—More Sweet—

A Hurrying Home of little Men
To Houses unperceived—
All this—and more—if I should tell—
Would never be believed—

Of Robins in the Trundle bed
How many I espy
Whose Nightgowns could not hide the Wings—
Although I heard them try—

But then I promised ne'er to tell—
How could I break My Word?
So go your Way—and I'll go Mine—
No fear you'll miss the Road.

425

Good Morning—Midnight—
I'm coming Home—
Day—got tired of Me—
How could I—of Him?

Sunshine was a sweet place—
I liked to stay—
But Morn—didn't want me—now—
So—Goodnight—Day!

I can look—can't I—
When the East is Red?
The Hills—have a way—then—
That puts the Heart—abroad—

You—are not so fair—Midnight—
I chose—Day—
But—please take a little Girl—
He turned away!

429

The Moon is distant from the Sea—
And yet, with Amber Hands—
She leads Him—docile as a Boy—
Along appointed Sands—

He never misses a Degree—
Obedient to Her Eye
He comes just so far—toward the Town—
Just so far—goes away—

Oh, Signor, Thine, the Amber Hand—
And mine—the distant Sea—
Obedient to the least command
Thine eye impose on me—

440

'Tis customary as we part
A trinket—to confer—
It helps to stimulate the faith
When Lovers be afar—

'Tis various—as the various taste—
Clematis—journeying far—
Presents me with a single Curl
Of her Electric Hair—

442

God made a little Gentian—
It tried—to be a Rose—
And failed—and all the Summer laughed—
But just before the Snows

There rose a Purple Creature—
That ravished all the Hill—
And Summer hid her Forehead—
And Mockery—was still—

The Frosts were her condition—
The Tyrian would not come
Until the North—invoke it—
Creator—Shall I—bloom?

492

Civilization—spurns—the Leopard!
Was the Leopard—bold?
Deserts—never rebuked her Satin—
Ethiop—her Gold—
Tawny—her Customs—
She was Conscious—
Spotted—her Dun Gown—
This was the Leopard's nature—Signor—
Need—a keeper—frown?

Pity—the Pard—that left her Asia—
Memories—of Palm—
Cannot be stifled—with Narcotic—
Nor suppressed—with Balm—

Within my Garden, rides a Bird
Upon a single Wheel—
Whose spokes a dizzy Music make
As 'twere a travelling Mill—

He never stops, but slackens
Above the Ripest Rose—
Partakes without alighting
And praises as he goes,

Till every spice is tasted—
And then his Fairy Gig
Reels in remoter atmospheres—
And I rejoin my Dog,

And He and I, perplex us
If positive, 'twere we—
Or bore the Garden in the Brain
This Curiosity—

But He, the best Logician,
Refers my clumsy eye—
To just vibrating Blossoms!
An Exquisite Reply!

507

She sights a Bird—she chuckles—
She flattens—then she crawls—
She runs without the look of feet—
Her eyes increase to Balls—

Her Jaws stir—twitching—hungry—
Her Teeth can hardly stand—
She leaps, but Robin leaped the first—
Ah, Pussy, of the Sand,

The Hopes so juicy ripening—
You almost bathed your Tongue—
When Bliss disclosed a hundred Toes—
And fled with every one—

526

To hear an Oriole sing
May be a common thing—
Or only a divine.

It is not of the Bird
Who sings the same, unheard,
As unto Crowd—

The Fashion of the Ear
Attireth that it hear
In Dun, or fair—

So whether it be Rune,
Or whether it be none
Is of within.

The "Tune is in the Tree—"
The Skeptic—showeth me—
"No Sir! In Thee!"

554

The Black Berry—wears a Thorn in his side—
But no Man heard Him cry—
He offers His Berry, just the same
To Partridge—and to Boy—

He sometimes holds upon the Fence—
Or struggles to a Tree—
Or clasps a Rock, with both His Hands—
But not for Sympathy—

We—tell a Hurt—to cool it—
This Mourner—to the Sky
A little further reaches—instead—
Brave Black Berry—

557

She hideth Her the last—
And is the first, to rise—
Her Night doth hardly recompense
The Closing of Her eyes—

She doth Her Purple Work—
And putteth Her away
In low Apartments in the Sod—
As Worthily as We.

To imitate Her life
As impotent would be
As make of Our imperfect Mints,
The Julep—of the Bee—

566

A Dying Tiger—moaned for Drink—
I hunted all the Sand—
I caught the Dripping of a Rock
And bore it in my Hand—

His Mighty Balls—in death were thick—
But searching—I could see
A Vision on the Retina
Of Water—and of me—

'Twas not my blame—who sped too slow—
'Twas not his blame—who died
While I was reaching him—
But 'twas—the fact that He was dead—

Of Brussels—it was not—
Of Kidderminster? Nay—
The Winds did buy it of the Woods—
They—sold it unto me

It was a gentle price—
The poorest—could afford—
It was within the frugal purse
Of Beggar—or of Bird—

Of small and spicy Yards—
In hue—a mellow Dun—
Of Sunshine—and of Sere—Composed—
But, principally—of Sun—

The Wind—unrolled it fast—
And spread it on the Ground—
Upholsterer of the Pines—is He—
Upholsterer—of the Pond—

605

The Spider holds a Silver Ball
In unperceived Hands—
And dancing softly to Himself
His Yarn of Pearl—unwinds—

He plies from Nought to Nought—
In unsubstantial Trade—
Supplants our Tapestries with His—
In half the period—

An Hour to rear supreme
His Continents of Light—
Then dangle from the Housewife's Broom—
His Boundaries—forgot—

634

You'll know Her—by Her Foot—
The smallest Gamboge Hand
With Fingers—where the Toes should be—
Would more affront the Sand—

Than this Quaint Creature's Boot—
Adjusted by a Stem—
Without a Button—I could vouch—
Unto a Velvet Limb—

You'll know Her—by Her Vest
Tight fitting—Orange—Brown—
Inside a Jacket duller—
She wore when she was born—

Her Cap is small—and snug—
Constructed for the Winds—
She'd pass for Barehead—short way off—
But as She Closer stands—

So finer 'tis than Wool—
You cannot feel the Seam—
Nor is it Clasped unto of Band—
Nor held upon—of Brim—

You'll know Her—by Her Voice—
At first—a doubtful Tone—
A sweet endeavor—but as March
To April—hurries on—

She squanders on your Ear
Such Arguments of Pearl—
You beg the Robin in your Brain
To keep the other—still—

671

She dwelleth in the Ground—
Where Daffodils—abide—
Her Maker—Her Metropolis—
The Universe—Her Maid—

To fetch Her Grace—and Hue—
And Fairness—and Renown—
The Firmament's—To Pluck Her—
And fetch Her Thee—be mine—

I could bring You Jewels—had I a mind to
But You have enough—of those—
I could bring You Odors from St. Domingo—
Colors—from Vera Cruz—

Berries of the Bahamas—have I—
But this little Blaze
Flickering to itself—in the Meadow—
Suits Me—more than those—

Never a Fellow matched this Topaz—
And his Emerald Swing—
Dower itself—for Bobadilo—
Better—Could I bring?

699

The Judge is like the Owl—
I've heard my Father tell—
And Owls do build in Oaks—
So here's an Amber Sill—

That slanted in my Path—
When going to the Barn—
And if it serve You for a House—
Itself is not in vain—

About the price—'tis small—
I only ask a Tune
At Midnight—Let the Owl select
His favorite Refrain.

No Bobolink—reverse His Singing
When the only Tree
Ever He minded occupying
By the Farmer be—

Clove to the Root—
His Spacious Future—
Best Horizon—gone—
Whose Music be His
Only Anodyne—
Brave Bobolink—

828

The Robin is the One
That interrupt the Morn
With hurried–few–express Reports
When March is scarcely on–

The Robin is the One
That overflow the Noon
With her cherubic quantity–
An April but begun–

The Robin is the One
That speechless from her Nest
Submit that Home–and Certainty
And Sanctity, are best

835

Nature and God—I neither knew
Yet Both so well knew me
They startled, like Executors
Of My identity.

Yet Neither told—that I could learn—
My Secret as secure
As Herschel's private interest
Or Mercury's affair—

Split the Lark—and you'll find the Music—
Bulb after Bulb, in Silver rolled—
Scantily dealt to the Summer Morning
Saved for your Ear when Lutes be old.

Loose the Flood—you shall find it patent—
Gush after Gush, reserved for you—
Scarlet Experiment! Sceptic Thomas!
Now, do you doubt that your Bird was true?

869

Because the Bee may blameless hum
For Thee a Bee do I become
List even unto Me.

Because the Flowers unafraid
May lift a look on thine, a Maid
Alway a Flower would be.

Nor Robins, Robins need not hide
When Thou upon their Crypts intrude
So Wings bestow on Me
Or Petals, or a Dower of Buzz
That Bee to ride, or Flower of Furze
I that way worship Thee.

872

As the Starved Maelstrom laps the Navies
As the Vulture teased
Forces the Broods in lonely Valleys
As the Tiger eased

By but a Crumb of Blood, fasts Scarlet
Till he meet a Man
Dainty adorned with Veins and Tissues
And partakes—his Tongue

Cooled by the Morsel for a moment
Grows a fiercer thing
Till he esteem his Dates and Cocoa
A Nutrition mean

I, of a finer Famine
Deem my Supper dry
For but a Berry of Domingo
And a Torrid Eye.

873

Ribbons of the Year—
Multitude Brocade—
Worn to Nature's Party once

Then, as flung aside
As a faded Bead
Or a Wrinkled Pearl
Who shall charge the Vanity
Of the Maker's Girl?

893

Drab Habitation of Whom?
Tabernacle or Tomb—
Or Dome of Worm—
Or Porch of Gnome—
Or some Elf's Catacomb?

927

Absent Place—an April Day—
Daffodils a-blow
Homesick curiosity
To the Souls that snow—

Drift may block within it
Deeper than without—
Daffodil delight but
Him it duplicate—

986

A narrow Fellow in the Grass
Occasionally rides—
You may have met Him—did you not
His notice sudden is—

The Grass divides as with a Comb—
A spotted shaft is seen—
And then it closes at your feet
And opens further on—

He likes a Boggy Acre
A Floor too cool for Corn—
Yet when a Boy, and Barefoot—
I more than once at Noon
Have passed, I thought, a Whip lash
Unbraiding in the Sun
When stooping to secure it
It wrinkled, and was gone—

Several of Nature's People
I know, and they know me—
I feel for them a transport
Of cordiality—

But never met this Fellow
Attended, or alone
Without a tighter breathing
And Zero at the Bone—

987

The Leaves like Women interchange
Exclusive Confidence—
Somewhat of nods and somewhat
Portentous inference.

The Parties in both cases
Enjoining secrecy—
Inviolable compact
To notoriety.

1009

I was a Phoebe—nothing more—
A Phoebe—nothing less—
The little note that others dropt
I fitted into place—

I dwelt too low that any seek—
Too shy, that any blame—
A Phoebe makes a little print
Upon the Floors of Fame—

His Bill an Auger is
His Head, a Cap and Frill
He laboreth at every Tree
A Worm, His utmost Goal.

1035

Bee! I'm expecting you!
Was saying Yesterday
To Somebody you know
That you were due—

The Frogs got Home last Week—
Are settled, and at work—
Birds, mostly back—
The Clover warm and thick—

You'll get my Letter by
The seventeenth; Reply
Or better, be with me—
Yours, Fly.

Her little Parasol to lift
And once to let it down
Her whole Responsibility–
To imitate be Mine.

A Summer further I must wear,
Content if Nature's Drawer
Present me from sepulchral Crease
As blemishless, as Her.

1086

What Twigs We held by—
Oh the View
When Life's swift River striven through
We pause before a further plunge
To take Momentum—
As the Fringe

Upon a former Garment shows
The Garment cast,
Our Props disclose
So scant, so eminently small
Of Might to help, so pitiful
To sink, if We had labored, fond
The diligence were not more blind

How scant, by everlasting Light
The Discs that satisfied Our Sight—
How dimmer than a Saturn's Bar
The Things esteemed, for Things that are!

Like Men and Women Shadows walk
Upon the Hills Today—
With here and there a mighty Bow
Or trailing Courtesy
To Neighbors doubtless of their own
Not quickened to perceive
Minuter landscape as Ourselves
And Boroughs where we live—

These are the Nights that Beetles love—
From Eminence remote
Drives ponderous perpendicular
His figure intimate
The terror of the Children
The merriment of men
Depositing his Thunder
He hoists abroad again—
A Bomb upon the Ceiling
Is an improving thing—
It keeps the nerves progressive
Conjecture flourishing—
Too dear the Summer evening
Without discreet alarm—
Supplied by Entomology
With its remaining charm—

1138

A Spider sewed at Night
Without a Light
Upon an Arc of White.

If Ruff it was of Dame
Or Shroud of Gnome
Himself himself inform.

Of Immortality
His Strategy
Was Physiognomy.

1167

Alone and in a Circumstance
Reluctant to be told
A spider on my reticence
Assiduously crawled

And so much more at Home than I
Immediately grew
I felt myself a visitor
And hurriedly withdrew

Revisiting my late abode
With articles of claim
I found it quietly assumed
As a Gymnasium
Where Tax asleep and Title off
The inmates of the Air
Perpetual presumption took
As each were special Heir—
If any strike me on the street
I can return the Blow—
If any take my property
According to the Law
The Statute is my Learned friend
But what redress can be
For an offense nor here nor there
So not in Equity—
That Larceny of time and mind
The marrow of the Day
By spider, or forbid it Lord
That I should specify.

A prompt—executive Bird is the Jay—
Bold as a Bailiff's Hymn—
Brittle and Brief in quality—
Warrant in every line—

Sitting a Bough like a Brigadier
Confident and straight—
Much is the mien of him in March
As a Magistrate—

1185

A little Dog that wags his tail
And knows no other joy
Of such a little Dog am I
Reminded by a Boy

Who gambols all the living Day
Without an earthly cause
Because he is little Boy
I honestly suppose—

The Cat that in the Corner dwells
Her martial Day forgot
The Mouse but a Tradition now
Of her desireless Lot

Another class remind me
Who neither please nor play
But not to make a "bit of noise"
Beseech each little Boy—

A Sparrow took a Slice of Twig
And thought it very nice
I think, because his empty Plate
Was handed Nature twice—

Invigorated, waded
In all the deepest Sky
Until his little Figure
Was forfeited away—

1232

The Clover's simple Fame
Remembered of the Cow—
Is better than enameled Realms
Of notability.
Renown perceives itself
And that degrades the Flower—
The Daisy that has looked behind
Has compromised its power—

1244

The Butterfly's Assumption Gown
In Chrysoprase Apartments hung
This afternoon put on—

How condescending to descend
And be of Buttercups the friend
In a New England Town—

1269

I worked for chaff and earning Wheat
Was haughty and betrayed.
What right had Fields to arbitrate
In matters ratified?

I tasted Wheat and hated Chaff
And thanked the ample friend—
Wisdom is more becoming viewed
At distance than at hand.

The Spider as an Artist
Has never been employed—
Though his surpassing Merit
Is freely certified

By every Broom and Bridget
Throughout a Christian Land—
Neglected Son of Genius
I take thee by the Hand—

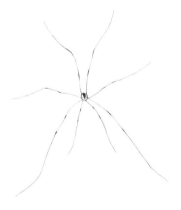

1276

'Twas later when the summer went
Than when the Cricket came—
And yet we knew that gentle Clock
Meant nought but Going Home—
'Twas sooner when the Cricket went
Than when the Winter came
Yet that pathetic Pendulum
Keeps esoteric Time.

The Way to know the Bobolink
From every other Bird
Precisely as the Joy of him—
Obliged to be inferred.

Of impudent Habiliment
Attired to defy,
Impertinence subordinate
At times to Majesty.

Of Sentiments seditious
Amenable to Law—
As Heresies of Transport
Or Puck's Apostacy.

Extrinsic to Attention
Too intimate with Joy—
He compliments existence
Until allured away

By Seasons or his Children—
Adult and urgent grown—
Or unforeseen aggrandizement
Or, happily, Renown—

By Contrast certifying
The Bird of Birds is gone—
How nullified the Meadow—
Her Sorcerer withdrawn!

1298

The Mushroom is the Elf of Plants—
At Evening, it is not—
At Morning, in a Truffled Hut
It stop upon a Spot

As if it tarried always
And yet its whole Career
Is shorter than a Snake's Delay
And fleeter than a Tare—

'Tis Vegetation's Juggler—
The Germ of Alibi—
Doth like a Bubble antedate
And like a Bubble, hie—

I feel as if the Grass was pleased
To have it intermit—
This surreptitious scion
Of Summer's circumspect.

Had Nature any supple Face
Or could she one contemn—
Had Nature an Apostate—
That Mushroom—it is Him!

Pink—small—and punctual—
Aromatic—low—
Covert—in April—
Candid—in May
Dear to the Moss—
Known to the Knoll—
Next to the Robin
In every human Soul—
Bold little Beauty
Bedecked with thee
Nature forswears
Antiquity—

1339

A Bee his burnished Carriage
Drove boldly to a Rose—
Combinedly alighting—
Himself—his Carriage was—
The Rose received his visit
With frank tranquillity
Withholding not a Crescent
To his Cupidity—
Their Moment consummated—
Remained for him—to flee—
Remained for her—of rapture
But the humility.

1340

A Rat surrendered here
A brief career of Cheer
And Fraud and Fear.

Of Ignominy's due
Let all addicted to
Beware.

The most obliging Trap
Its tendency to snap
Cannot resist—

Temptation is the Friend
Repugnantly resigned
At last.

1343

A single Clover Plank
Was all that saved a Bee
A Bee I personally knew
From sinking in the sky—

'Twixt Firmament above
And Firmament below
The Billows of Circumference
Were sweeping him away—

The idly swaying Plank
Responsible to nought
A sudden Freight of Wind assumed
And Bumble Bee was not—

This harrowing event
Transpiring in the Grass
Did not so much as wring from him
A wandering "Alas"—

1356

The Rat is the concisest Tenant.
He pays no Rent.
Repudiates the Obligation—
On Schemes intent

Balking our Wit
To sound or circumvent—
Hate cannot harm
A Foe so reticent—
Neither Decree prohibit him—
Lawful as Equilibrium.

1359

The long sigh of the Frog
Upon a Summer's Day
Enacts intoxication
Upon the Revery—
But his receding Swell
Substantiates a Peace
That makes the Ear inordinate
For corporal release—

1393

Lay this Laurel on the One
Too intrinsic for Renown—
Laurel—veil your deathless tree—
Him you chasten, that is He!

After all Birds have been investigated and laid aside—
Nature imparts the little Blue-Bird—assured
Her conscientious Voice will soar unmoved
Above ostensible Vicissitude.

First at the March—competing with the Wind—
Her panting note exalts us—like a friend—
Last to adhere when Summer cleaves away—
Elegy of Integrity.

1423

The fairest Home I ever knew
Was founded in an Hour
By Parties also that I knew
A spider and a Flower—
A manse of mechlin and of Floss—

1424

The Gentian has a parched Corolla—
Like azure dried
'Tis Nature's buoyant juices
Beatified—
Without a vaunt or sheen
As casual as Rain
And as benign—

When most is past—it comes—
Nor isolate it seems
Its Bond its Friend—
To fill its Fringed career
And aid an aged Year
Abundant end—

Its lot—were it forgot—
This Truth endear—
Fidelity is gain
Creation o'er—

1437

A Dew sufficed itself—
And satisfied a Leaf
And felt "how vast a destiny"—
"How trivial is Life!"

The Sun went out to work—
The Day went out to play
And not again that Dew be seen
By Physiognomy

Whether by Day Abducted
Or emptied by the Sun
Into the Sea in passing
Eternally unknown

Attested to this Day
That awful Tragedy
By Transport's instability
And Doom's celerity.

1448

How soft a Caterpillar steps—
I find one on my Hand
From such a velvet world it comes
Such plushes at command
Its soundless travels just arrest
My slow—terrestrial eye
Intent upon its own career
What use has it for me—

1463

A Route of Evanescence
With a revolving Wheel—
A Resonance of Emerald—
A Rush of Cochineal—
And every Blossom on the Bush
Adjusts its tumbled Head—
The mail from Tunis, probably,
An easy Morning's Ride—

Before you thought of Spring
Except as a Surmise
You see—God bless his suddenness—
A Fellow in the Skies
Of independent Hues
A little weather worn
Inspiriting habiliments
Of Indigo and Brown—
With specimens of Song
As if for you to choose—
Discretion in the interval
With gay delays he goes
To some superior Tree
Without a single Leaf
And shouts for joy to Nobody
But his seraphic self—

One of the ones that Midas touched
Who failed to touch us all
Was that confiding Prodigal
The reeling Oriole—

So drunk he disavows it
With badinage divine—
So dazzling we mistake him
For an alighting Mine—

A Pleader—a Dissembler—
An Epicure—a Thief—
Betimes an Oratorio—
An Ecstasy in chief—

The Jesuit of Orchards
He cheats as he enchants
Of an entire Attar
For his decamping wants—

The splendor of a Burmah
The Meteor of Birds,
Departing like a Pageant
Of Ballads and of Bards—

I never thought that Jason sought
For any Golden Fleece
But then I am a rural man
With thoughts that make for Peace—

But if there were a Jason,
Tradition bear with me
Behold his lost Aggrandizement
Upon the Apple Tree—

1468

A winged spark doth soar about—
I never met it near
For Lightning it is oft mistook
When nights are hot and sere—

Its twinkling Travels it pursues
Above the Haunts of men—
A speck of Rapture—first perceived
By feeling it is gone—
Rekindled by some action quaint

The Robin is a Gabriel
In humble circumstances—
His Dress denotes him socially,
Of Transport's Working Classes—
He has the punctuality
Of the New England Farmer—
The same oblique integrity,
A Vista vastly warmer—

A small but sturdy Residence,
A self denying Household,
The Guests of Perspicacity
Are all that cross his Threshold—
As covert as a Fugitive,
Cajoling Consternation
By Ditties to the Enemy
And Sylvan Punctuation—

1500

It came his turn to beg—
The begging for the life
Is different from another Alms
'Tis Penury in Chief—

I scanned his narrow realm
I gave him leave to live
Lest Gratitude revive the snake
Though smuggled his reprieve

1501

Its little Ether Hood
Doth sit upon its Head—
The millinery supple
Of the sagacious God—

Till when it slip away
A nothing at a time—
And Dandelion's Drama
Expires in a stem.

1514

An Antiquated Tree
Is cherished of the Crow
Because that Junior Foliage is disrespectful now
To venerable Birds
Whose Corporation Coat
Would decorate Oblivion's
Remotest Consulate.

1519

The Dandelion's pallid tube
Astonishes the Grass,
And Winter instantly becomes
An infinite Alas—
The tube uplifts a signal Bud
And them a shouting Flower,—
The Proclamation of the Suns
That sepulture is o'er.

1526

His oriental heresies
Exhilarate the Bee,
And filling all the Earth and Air
With gay apostasy

Fatigued at last, a Clover plain
Allures his jaded eye
That lowly Breast where Butterflies
Have felt it meet to die—

1538

Follow wise Orion
Till you waste your Eye—
Dazzingly decamping
He is just as high—

1542

Come show thy Durham Breast
To her who loves thee best,
Delicious Robin—
And if it be not me
At least within my Tree
Do the avowing—
Thy Nuptial so minute
Perhaps is more astute
Than vaster suing—
For so to soar away
Is our propensity
The Day ensuing—

No Brigadier throughout the Year
So civic as the Jay—
A Neighbor and a Warrior too
With shrill felicity
Pursuing Winds that censure us
A February Day,
The Brother of the Universe
Was never blown away—
The Snow and he are intimate—
I've often seen them play
When Heaven looked upon us all
With such severity
I felt apology were due
To an insulted sky
Whose pompous frown was Nutriment
To their Temerity—
The Pillow of this daring Head
Is pungent Evergreens—
His Larder—terse and Militant—
Unknown—refreshing things—
His Character—a Tonic—
His Future—a Dispute—
Unfair an Immortality
That leaves this Neighbor out—

1570

Forever honored be the Tree
Whose Apple Winterworn
Enticed to Breakfast from the Sky
Two Gabriels Yestermorn.

They registered in Nature's Book
As Robins—Sire and Son—
But Angels have that modest way
To screen them from Renown.

1575

The Bat is dun, with wrinkled Wings—
Like fallow Article—
And not a song pervade his Lips—
Or none perceptible.

His small Umbrella quaintly halved
Describing in the Air
An Arc alike inscrutable
Elate Philosopher.

Deputed from what Firmament—
Of what Astute Abode—
Empowered with what Malignity
Auspiciously withheld—

To his adroit Creator
Ascribe no less the praise—
Beneficent, believe me,
His Eccentricities—

1581

The farthest Thunder that I heard
Was nearer than the Sky
And rumbles still, though torrid Noons
Have lain their missiles by—
The Lightning that preceded it
Struck no one but myself—
But I would not exchange the Bolt
For all the rest of Life—
Indebtedness to Oxygen
The Happy may repay,
But not the obligation
To Electricity—
It founds the Homes and decks the Days
And every clamor bright
Is but the gleams concomitant
Of that waylaying Light—
The Thought is quiet as a Flake—
A Crash without a Sound,
How Life's reverberation
Its Explanation found—

The Bobolink is gone—
The Rowdy of the Meadow—
And no one swaggers now but me—
The Presbyterian Birds
Can now resume the Meeting
He boldly interrupted that overflowing Day
When supplicating mercy
In a portentous way
He swung upon the Decalogue
And shouted let us pray—

1624

Apparently with no surprise
To any happy Flower
The Frost beheads it at its play—
In accidental power—
The blonde Assassin passes on—
The Sun proceeds unmoved
To measure off another Day
For an Approving God.

1627

The Pedigree of Honey
Does not concern the Bee—
A Clover, any time, to him,
Is Aristocracy—

1635

The Jay his Castanet has struck
Put on your muff for Winter
The Tippet that ignores his voice
Is impudent to nature

Of Swarthy Days he is the close
His Lotus is a chestnut
The Cricket drops a sable line
No more from yours at present

1649

A Cap of Lead across the sky
Was tight and surly drawn
We could not find the mighty Face
The Figure was withdrawn—

A Chill came up as from a shaft
Our noon became a well
A Thunder storm combines the charms
Of Winter and of Hell.

1740

Sweet is the swamp with its secrets,
Until we meet a snake;
'Tis then we sigh for houses,
And our departure take
At that enthralling gallop
That only childhood knows.
A snake is summer's treason,
And guile is where it goes.

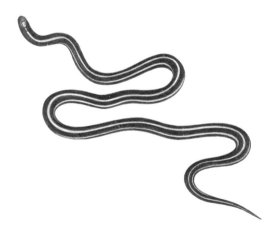

1755

To make a prairie it takes a clover and one bee,
One clover, and a bee,
And revery.
The revery alone will do,
If bees are few.

ACKNOWLEDGMENTS

I would like to thank Karen Dane, Carol Judy Leslie, Melissa Lotfy, Ann Eiselein, Josh Marwell, Robyn Renahan, Becky Hemperly, and Ken Wong, all from Little, Brown and Company / Bulfinch Press, designer Christopher Kuntze, and everyone at The Stinehour Press for their excellent work and dedication to this poetry series.

Ferris Cook
High Falls, New York
December 19, 1997

Book design by Christopher Kuntze
Printed by The Stinehour Press, Lunenburg, Vermont
Bound by Acme Bookbinding, Charlestown, Massachusetts